My

Red

Sneakers

Darlene Chambers

In memory of:

My Heavenly sister Sharlene, who was my best
friend in all these memories, and to my Mother,
who was my everything.

And to my dear sisters with love and
happiness at how strong we all
have become.

Preface

I had this idea about writing this book for a few years. When I was working nights at the hospital, sometimes my assignment would be taking care of only one patient at a time. When they fell asleep and I would be sitting there in the darkness of their room, I would spend my time writing down my memories of my childhood. I always kept a large pad of paper in my backpack and a pen ready to go at any time.

One day I had a bottle of water that spilled out and got everything in my bag soaked. Not thinking about my memoir, I threw everything out that had gotten wet. Later, I remembered!!!! Oh my goodness, my book! Oh no, what did I do. *I threw it away!* But, no problem because all I had to do was start writing it all over again. Everything was in my head and had been there and was not going anywhere. So, I started writing everything down on a new large pad of paper. It just flowed out of my head through my arm to my pen onto the paper. Once I started, I couldn't stop. I'm hoping my family and friends will love my stories as much as I loved writing them.

Letting my family know about my mother when she was only in her twenties and my father when he was in his thirties is very important to me. Dad died in a motorcycle accident that killed him in his forties. Mom died in her eighties with memory loss, which was heart breaking to me. To lose your memory of who you are and where you came from and how you got to be the person that you are. How sad that must have been for her and for so many people that have gone through the same thing. So, I knew I had to do this book.

My Red Sneakers

This book is about my memories, from around three years old to about nine years old. It was a special time for me, and it formed me into the person that I am today. This book is written from a little girl's point of view.

I want to say a Heavenly Thank-you to my Grammy Chambers. Every time we visited her in Red Beach, Maine after we moved to Exeter, she would apologize for only having warm biscuits and homemade jam for us to eat. I still can picture her by her kitchen stove, which was heated by wood, warming the biscuits on the top of the cast iron. Her with her apron around her belly and her sweet smile with her silver hair in a little bun on the back of her head. It still is my favorite thing to eat, biscuits and jam with a cup of tea.

Since I was that little girl in those deep woods of Maine, my life has been full of challenges. A lot of ups and downs for sure. But, that little innocent girl has always stayed with me in my heart. She is precious to me, her curiosity and love for every living thing.

I know that my life has been full, and I feel very spoiled now. I have many shoes to go with different outfits in my closet. Even some that I have never worn yet. I have heat in every room, I have lights, bright lights whenever I want them, and I have running water, too. Still, every time that I turn on a faucet my heart races when I hear the water coming out. I think about where that water comes from and my little well in Maine.

I hope you enjoy my story!

Love to you all, Huggs and Kisses...

Darlene

One

This is a book that I'm writing about my childhood. It was so precious and I don't want it to be forgotten. It's going to be about me, Darlene, and my two younger sisters, Sharlene and Judy Mae. I was a little, toe-headed girl. That's what they called me because I had very blond hair. I always thought it was very strange that people called me that because it had nothing to do with toes.

The time was in the early 1950s, where men ruled the home. Women stayed at home and took care of their husband, children, and the house. Women did what the men wanted and took care of their every need. Even as a little girl I knew that Dad was in charge, and we had to obey both him and Mom and that was the way it was!

My father, Percy, was one of twelve children, so I had a lot of uncles and aunts living all around us in little seacoast towns. His father, Ralph Chambers, and mother, Jenny, lived in a small town named Red Beach where the rocks near the ocean were pink until the waves hit them and then they were a beautiful red. I loved to go to Grammy's just to see those beautiful rocks. I really wanted to stop and put them in my pockets and take some home with me, but I never told Dad that. So, I would just smell the ocean air and look at the beautiful rocks while we drove by. I thought to myself that someday I'll bring home one of those rocks to keep. Someday!

I knew that Dad loved his family so much. When he was around them, he would be so happy. He smiled a lot and was very talkative, and he would laugh, too. I loved watching him because he was so different at Grammy's than when he was home with us. He would see me watching everyone and he would snap his fingers and tell me and my sisters to go outside and play. I loved it outside at Grammy's because I could smell the ocean and she had beautiful green grass and it felt so soft on my feet.

At home, Dad never talked to us much. He would just tell us to go away. Really, Mom didn't talk to us much and she hardly ever smiled either. I always thought she was just too busy to play with me. But, when Dad wasn't there, Mom would smile more and that made me so happy. I always knew that Mom was scared of Dad, like I was, and she wanted to be loved, too. All I knew was that I had to be a good little girl and do what Dad and Mom wanted. It didn't always work out that way. I tried my hardest to stay away from him, but I wanted him to love me and see that I was good. He was very stern, and his voice was loud and aggressive. When he looked at me it frightened me, and I didn't like it. He would slap his big hard hands on the table to get our attention and sometimes he would snap his fingers at us so we would look at him. I would get so nervous. I was so afraid of him, and I didn't know what he was going to do next. I would try and try to be a good little girl so he would love me instead of hitting me. Why? Why would he pull my pants down and spank me with his hard hands. What did I do that was so bad? Why? Sometimes even with his belt! Oh my goodness, when I saw him pulling his belt out of his pants I would get so scared. He would fold the belt in half and snap the leather together to make this loud sound and I knew I was in trouble. Sometimes he would tell me to go outside and pick out my own switch for him to use. He said he liked the long ones with little pieces of wood still attached to it. Those ones really hurt!!!

I knew that If I stayed outside and played it

was going to be my safe place and I loved playing with my sisters so much.

Now my mom, Beverly, was the only child of Shirley and Erving Sherman. Mom was from a broken marriage, which was unheard of in the 50s. Mom used to say that she was very spoiled and wanted for nothing. She told me that Grammy had introduced her to Dad and that Grammy thought Dad was very cute. Her mother, Shirley (which I'm named after, Darlene Shirley), had remarried and we didn't see her much. Dad didn't like her new husband, Dougal Dana, because he was a Native American from the Quoddy Village and Grammy new it. Mom's grandmother loved Mom so much that when Mom got married, she gave them her home as long as she got to stay there.

Two

We lived in a small town in down east Maine, named Robbinston. We live in a small wooden house that belonged to my great grandmother, Alice Diffen. My great grandmother lived with us, along with my mother and father, and my sisters: Sharlene and Judy Mae.

I was the oldest of my sisters, but I don't remember life without them in it. So, the beginning of my memories started at age three.

Our house was on a dirt road with no neighbors, just a lot of trees. On the main road there was a blue house that I could see from our house. Mom said that she grew up in that little blue house. I loved looking at it and thinking about Mom as a little girl like me, playing and having fun in the sun.

My mother was always in the house taking care of my great grandmother. Helping her get dressed and going to pee in a very small pot on the floor called a chamber pot. I wasn't suppose to be peeking, but I could hear a commotion going on in Grammy's living room so I had to look and see what was going. Mom had a very hard time getting Grammy off the pee pot that was on the floor. She had Grammy's hands in hers and was trying to pull her up to a standing position. They were laughing and smiling at each other because of the predicament that they were having. They were laughing so hard because they didn't want to spill the chamber pot. I thought while watching them, *Poor Mom and Grammy. What are they going to do?* Mom loved her grandmother so much and I knew that. I could feel it in my heart, and it always made me so happy to see them together. My great grandmother enjoyed making things with her hands: knitting, crocheting, quilting and she loved reading, too. Our home was full of love for each other. I used to watch Mom taking care of my great grandmother. Washing her, combing her hair, and getting her dressed. Really doing everything for her. Mom was such a great person, taking care of Grammy and with three little ones and a husband, too.

The house had very little electricity. I think only one line came into the kitchen from outside.

We had no running water. Just a well and an outhouse. We only had a wood stove in the living room and a wood cooking stove in the kitchen to heat the whole house. I loved the smell of the wood burning and the heat that came out of that stove felt so nice. It was so warm, and I loved being near it. The house was small, which was a good thing.

We had an outhouse to use. It got very hot in

there in the summertime and very stinky, too. I never stayed in there for long. At nighttime, my sisters and I had a white porcelain chamber pot to use. It was on the floor at the foot of our bed. It had a cover on it so it wasn't so bad, but it was very cold on my fanny in the winter time.

My sisters and I used to sleep in the same bedroom upstairs. There was a hole in the floor of each bedroom with a beautiful black metal grate that would let the heat come up from the kitchen stove and it would heat the upstairs. My sisters and I liked looking down the hole to see Mom making breakfast and feeling the heat on our little faces. The smell was so wonderful, and it was fun watching Mom move around so fast. I always thought she didn't know we were watching her, and I thought it was fun to be so secretive. But no matter what, we had to stay upstairs until Mom called us down to eat. She didn't want us in her way while she was getting her day started. We would go down the stairs slowly. Back then the stairs were narrow and steep, and they had a bend halfway down. I always thought they were kinda scary. The table would be all set up with our own bowls and cups. We all had our own colored dishes.

Mom would get us ready to go outside so she could get her work done and we wouldn't be in her way.

We would get dressed fast and stand in line and she would brush our hair and put it in braids or a ponytail. Sometimes we would get pigtails. Mom brushed so hard and so fast it would hurt. I thought to myself that she didn't have much time to get us out of the house.

I loved it outside. The sun was warm and all the sounds! It was a wonderful place. So much to explore and so much to do.

I slept with pillows that were full of chicken feathers, but I didn't know it. My pillow would be a little lumpy and sometimes scratchy. Every once in a while, something very sharp would be poking out of my pillow and it would hurt me while I slept. I would wake up and start to pull it out slowly and a feather would slip out into my hand. I was so surprised to know that my pillow was full of beautiful, colorful feathers! So, over time, if I felt something poking me I would pull it out and marvel over the beauty of it. I put them all in my drawer in my bedroom and I would look at my collection that was growing. Every one was different and so wonderful all by themselves. I was so lucky to have a collection of feathers so soft and light.

Every early spring Mom would have me go around and pick the dandelion leaves. She showed me which ones to pick and which ones not to pick. She said to only pick the new fresh leaves, not the old leaves that were there all winter. Mom would take the leaves I gave her and smile at me. She cooked them up for supper and they tasted so good.

My Red Sneakers

When it rained, the roof would leak. Mom hurried and got her pots and pans, and I would help her to put them on the floor to keep the water in. I knew mom was so serious but I loved helping her and my job was watching the pans fill up and telling her so she could empty them. The sound was like music to me coming from all parts of the little upstairs.

We didn't have running water, but we had our own well. It was made out of rocks, and it had a long rope and a bucket. Mom had me and Sharlene go fetch her some water every day. I tried my best. I was the oldest and the biggest, so I had to work the hardest. When I looked down the well it was so dark. It smelled so good. My face felt cooler than the air around me. It was very nice. I filled the bucket in the well with water and poured the water into my bucket to bring to Mom. I walked so carefully, but the water kept spilling out on my legs. By the time I got to the house, the pail would be half empty and my pants would be wet. I was always sad that I lost a lot of the water. I thought next time I would do better for Mom.

We had a mean dog on a chain that was hooked up to a doghouse near the well. We had to go around him to get to the well, and when he saw us, he would run so fast that his chain was out straight and he wouldn't stop barking the whole time. We would have to get the water while he was barking at us. I was scared of him. I never touched him because he had big white teeth! I don't know why we even had him because he wasn't friendly at all. Maybe because he was supposed to let us know if someone or something was coming! I don't know but he was so big and mean.

I would be running as fast as I could go and screaming all the way to the well. I could hear the chain dragging thew the dry dirt around the doghouse until the chain was tight while he continued to bark in a cloud of dust. I was safe!

My Red Sneakers

We had chickens, and Sharlene and I had our own roosters. My rooster was big and very colorful. It had a very big tail and so did Sharlene's. Judy had a fat chicken. I never could catch my rooster, but I thought how pretty he was in the sun. His feathers were so sparkly and shiny and he would walk so proud and tall all around the yard.

We always had heavy winter blankets on our little beds. They weighed us down but made us so warm. It was hard to get out of bed because it was so cold in our bedroom that we could see our breath. If we had to go pee, we had a little white pot on the floor to go in. Mom would bring it out to the outhouse after making the beds, to get ready for the next night.

Our blankets were all handmade by Great Grammy and Mom out of old wool clothes and old scraps of wool material. I always knew when spring was coming, because Mom changed our blankets to lighter ones. But, I always missed the heavy ones. There was something about the weight that made me feel safe and loved.

We would get government beans and cheese and peanut butter. We had so many beans that Mom had them in a room and the mice would get into them. I thought this was really funny how Mom made the mice so happy.

Mom was a great cook. She made everything from scratch. She didn't know how to cook before she got married, so she had a lot to learn. Dad taught her a lot and they would laugh about it and all her mistakes. I'm sure Grammy taught her a lot, too, but Dad always took the credit for it. Mom never wanted us to be inside while she was cooking, so this was the beginning of my love for the outdoors and nature.

We had three old apple trees in a row, so Dad made swings in each of the trees out of wood and rope. One each for me, Sharlene, and Judy. We loved those swings, and we would swing every day in the warmer weather. I tried to use my legs and go high, but the ropes were so long that it never would go very high. I would pump and pump my legs over and over again. I loved my swing but sometimes it made me feel sick if I played on it too long and I went too high.

We had old apple trees that had large yellow apples on them. Mom would have me pick them for her so she could make apple pies. While I was outside playing, I could smell the pies cooling on the windowsill.

We also had a plum tree. They were so delicious. Mom would see me eating them from the kitchen window and she needed them for her jams. I loved Mom's jams but I loved those plums.

She would holler to me, "Darlene, stop eating my plums or you will get a bellyache!" So I would hide behind the tree and get a plum and run and eat it. And she was right, I did get a bellyache and ended up in the outhouse a lot!!!! I loved eating the flowers that grew wild around me. If the bees loved them so would I. At least this is what

My Red Sneakers

I thought! There was an orange flower that was everywhere and early in the mornings there would be a dewdrop of juice on the end of the flower. I was so happy when I saw that. I sucked on each flower and tasted the sweetness of the flower nectar. I would go from one flower to the next till I was full.

There were also these white flowers that made these wonderful seeds. When I saw the mature seeds on the flowers, I would eat them, too. They were so spicy and delicious. I think now that they were caraway seeds. I'm very lucky I didn't eat anything that was poison. I loved the taste of thick green grasses and the little green round head that was on a weed that was everywhere. I watched people walking on them, not knowing that they were so tasty.

We had a veggie garden in the hot sun. I can only remember the cucumbers, but Dad planted other vegetables too. I was told to keep the garden weeded. I hated to do it. My hands would get so dirty and dry. It was so hot in the sun, too. I had to go inside to get some water. Mom would put a dipper into the bucket she kept by her sink and would give me a drink from it. It was cool and tasted so good. Mom told me to get back outside to play and I did.

Mom's sink in the kitchen had a pipe that stuck outside the house. When mom put water in the sink to wash the dishes it would pour out the pipe when she was done and end up outside on the ground. They called it "gray water." You would not believe the wildflowers that grew in the gray water. And the bees and bugs that lived in that area. It was so full of life and noise. The ground was never dry. The bumblebees were so big and the butterflies were so colorful. I would set and watch them all day.

One day, I had this great idea. I found an old fork in the woods (We had our own dump in the woods. It was full of *everything*). I ripped up one of those wildflowers with the roots still attached and full of bumblebees. I laid it carefully down on its side on the ground. The bees were so busy getting the pollen off the flowers they never noticed me. So, carefully, I stuck the fork into a bee and brought it close so I could see it better and it would stay still. The bee was so fat and beautiful. The wings were so pretty and see-through. The legs had piles of pollen on them. Wow, how lucky I was to see all of this but how do I get the bee off so it could go home? I took my finger up to the bee and tried to get him off the fork, but he stung me. It hurt so bad! I never played with bees again, but I still loved watching them from a distance.

I had a club house "for girls only" under the large cluster of lilac bushes. These were Great Grammy's favorite flowers and the bushes of lilac were so big and long. They grew along the side of the house in the front yard.

I loved it there. It was like my own house. I kept it very clean and neat. I swept the ground so much that the dirt had no leaves on it and the dirt was very smooth and hard.

Each home in Maine had their own dump in the backyard. It was great because I could find so many things in that dump. One day, I even found potatoes growing. I was so happy, and I ran inside to tell Mom about my find. She just smiled at me, and I went back outside to investigate for more treasures. I went into the woods and found a double outhouse seat. All the outhouses I ever went into had only one hole but this one was long and had two holes. It was very old and weathered because it was in the woods for so long and it was a deep gray color wood. It was so perfect and it didn't smell! I dragged it into my clubhouse and used it for a kitchen sink. It was a double setter and so I used both holes and I loved my kitchen. I would make a lot of mud pies and put flowers on the tops of them. I would work on them for hours just like Mom in her kitchen. They were so pretty and perfect sitting side by side. Then, after I pretended to eat them (they were so good), I would clean my pie plates off and dump everything down the sink. Then the floor would be messy again so I would have to sweep the floor again. I would cook every day and sweep every day. I thought that a girl's work is never done. This all made me so happy to be so busy in my special little secret place under all those flowers and leaves.

The neighbor boys wanted to come into my club house and play with me and my sisters. They were kinda naughty when they would come around, so I didn't like that idea at all! They always wanted to pull down their pants and show us something. One time they got up in a tree and their pee pee thing was sticking out and I thought it was a hotdog and it scared me so much. I didn't like those boys and I wanted them to go home! So, I made a big sign that said, "NO BOYS ALLOWED" and placed it against the lilac bushes facing their house. It worked! They never came in. It was so private and special. I could hear the bees and birds all around me. I was so happy playing in my house.

Three

One day I was playing in a field of daisies. The field was full of flowers that were up to my waist. I danced and sang church songs as I was running through the field. There was a puddle of water and mud from a shower that we had the night before. I didn't see it and I stepped right into it and got my shoes and socks wet and muddy. I started crying because Mom would be very mad at me. My neighbor Marlene heard me and came over and helped me. She was a few years older than me and I loved her. I thought she was so pretty and mature. She was those bad boys' big sister. She took off my wet shoes and socks and cleaned them in a clean puddle. I thought she was so smart. Then she placed my shoes and socks on the tops of some flowers and let the sun dry them out. I spent the day laying down in the field of flowers waiting for them to dry. While I was laying there no one could see me. I loved the feeling of hiding in the flowers. The sun was so warm on my face and again the flowers were full of singing bees. The flowers moved with the breeze side to side. I laid there and watched them moving and every once in a while a butterfly would fly by. I was so happy. Mom never knew about anything when I went into the house that night and I went to bed happy.

Four

Somedays Mom would bring out this galvanized round tub early in the morning and placed it on the ground. Then she went to the well and filled it up with water. She wanted the summer sun to heat up the water. She would come out now and then to feel it. I knew what was coming, and I would be so excited for Mom to say, "It's ready girls! Get in!!!" So I took all my clothes off and jumped in with Sharlene and Judy. We thought it was like being at a lake. We had a great time bathing and getting clean outside in the sun.

In the winter, Mom would place the tub beside

the woodstove to heat up the water. I loved that, too. Feeling the heat of the stove while I was taking a bath. We did this about once a week and I always loved taking a bath in my little tub.

The first time I saw a porcelain claw tub was after we had moved to Exeter and I was about nine years old. It was pink on the outside and white and shiny inside with a little rust stain from the water by the drain. I had never taken a bath in so much water before. I didn't want to waste all that water so I wouldn't fill it up very high, but when I did, it was like I was swimming. So much water just coming out of a faucet filling up the tub. So easy and so nice. It wasn't like it was in Maine for sure. I think I liked running water!

Five

Dad would take us to visit Grammy and Grandpa Chambers often. Dad's father, Ralph, always sat in a brown leather chair by the window with a rolled up newspaper in his big hands just waiting to kill a fly. There were dead flies all over the windows which I loved to study after he left his chair.

My sister and I would play in his chair, which people called a Murphy chair. It had a steel pole in the back and you could move it up or down to recline the chair. We loved to play in his chair so much, as long as he wasn't around to see us.

Grandpa wasn't really a talker for someone

that had twelve children. I really felt that he didn't like us much. When he came into the kitchen to sit in his chair, we would run and he would tell us to go outside to play, which was fine with me. Yay!

Outside, Grammy had a water pump in her back-yard. I loved playing with it and I wished we had one like that in our yard. It would make life a lot easier. I would pump the handle up and down till rusty water would come squirting out. I would put a water pail on the nozzle to catch the clear water then bring it into Grammy's house. She would smile at me and say, "Thank-you Miss Darlene." Grammy also had a well, but you had to go down the road a bit. It had a board to cover it so the leaves and dirt didn't get inside the well and it would keep the water clean. I thought it was a good idea. It was a deep well but not as deep as our well was at home and it was further away from her home, too. By the time I walked up the road and up her long driveway I was soaked with the splashing water from the bucket.

We never had company come over. Maybe people knew that Dad wasn't always very nice. So, it was always a treat to visit Grammy and Grandpa and my aunts and uncles. When we got to their homes, Dad would make us sit in a row and we couldn't talk.

The people were so happy to see us. They had pretty furniture and a lot of rugs and their house was so big with a lot of rooms. The windows were very large, and the front door was so beautiful with large wooden steps going inside. They had wallpaper with bright flowers and dishes everywhere. Dad would tell us that when we got there, we were to be seen but not heard. One time, this lady brought out this big bowl of homemade cookies. I love cookies and we didn't have them at home much. I saw that dish with all those cookies and my mouth started to water with the thought of them. They asked us if we wanted a cookie, well we all were so excited, but Dad stood behind them and looked at us and shook his head NO! We would see him and we all said at the same time, no thank you. People always thought we were so cute to do that but it always made me sad. I really wanted a cookie so badly, but doing what Dad wanted was the right thing to do. They always tried to change our minds but we knew we couldn't because of Dad. Dad was pleased that we all did what he wanted us to do, but I bet those homemade cookies were good.

Some of my uncles and aunts still lived with Grammy and Grandpa. Sometimes when we visited, Dad would go off with his brothers and leave us behind. They would come back with buckets full of crabs. Grammy would cook them and bring outside a whole bucket of cooked crabs for me and my sisters to eat.

We would set in the sun on this big rock that looked like an elephant's back popping out of the ground, with our bucket of cooked crabs. We would take small rocks and break open those crabs and eat every one. It was so fun being at Grammy's house doing fun stuff with my cousins. Sometimes it was just fun laying on blankets in the shade on the side of the house talking. Well, I really didn't talk much but I enjoyed listening to my older cousins talking about stuff that I didn't know anything about.

One time they told me that the pitch on the side of the tree was gum. I didn't think so, but they were older and wiser than me. They got a knife from the house and cut me off a piece. I started chewing it and it tasted awful, but they said, "Darlene keep chewing and it will get better." But, it never did and I spit it out. They laughed at me, and I laughed, too.

We didn't always have a car so Dad's brother and sisters would bring my dad places. But, we did have this old model T Ford in our yard which was black and I loved it! The seats looked so comfortable. Dad saw me looking at it and he would tell me over and over again not to go near that car ever.

One day, I planned it out how to get up in that car and pretend that I was driving it. Dad was nowhere around, so I slowly stood on the running board and YES, it was a bad idea. My weight broke that rusty metal and cut my leg bad. I HAD TO GO INSIDE AND SHOW THEM MY BLOODY LEG!!!! Oh no, I knew I was going to get into so much trouble and the belt would come out! I looked at Dad and told him that I fell on a sharp rock and hurt myself. Dad made me go outside and point out to him which rock it was. I looked everywhere at every rock in the front yard, but I couldn't find a pointy one. Dad knew I was lying, and he knew I had climbed on that old rusty car. I was in big trouble and my leg was so bloody that it was dripping all over the yard. Dad ran to the neighbors' house, and they took us to the doctors. Dad was sitting in the front set laughing and telling me that the doctor was going to sew me up with a big needle and thread. I was so scared, but the doctor was very nice to me and I didn't feel a thing. I never played on that car again.

Six

Nature was everywhere and I was so fascinated with the beauty. I would ask Mom for paper, but we didn't always have any. But, we always had paper bags! I thought that would work just fine. Mom would give me this little pencil and away I went. Dad saw my drawings and thought I traced it from something. I was so happy that he thought that, because that meant it must of been a good drawing. Mom told him tracing was impossible because the bag was so thick. I never stopped drawing and coloring.

One of my favorite things to draw was this beautiful house with shrubs and flowers around it. It had a big tree in the front yard and a lot of green grass. I used to draw the same picture over and over again. It was a picture that was always in my head, so when I was older, I actually built that house and made those gardens that I use to draw all those years ago. It was so wonderful to see it and live in it.

I also became a full-time artist as an adult and my mind goes back to those times when I had that freedom to explore the outside world. How lucky my childhood was to be me.

Seven

We didn't have tissues like today. We had handkerchiefs. My mom made them for us. She had me draw a butterfly in the corner of each handkerchief for me and each of my sisters. She showed us all her colored floss to embroider the butterflies with. She would pull out her basket, made out of sweetgrass, and pull off the cover and show us what was inside. It was full of threads that were all different. Her basket was full of colors. We all would look into her basket and touch them. She said that we could have our butterflies be any color we wanted. It was so pretty and so fun to pick out the colors. It was so hard to decide on only two colors, but I did. I picked yellow and purple. I wish I still had that hankie!

When it was getting colder outside, and winter was around the corner, Mom would make our winter coats for us. My Great Grammy had a lot of old coats, and she would give up some of her old coats for us. If we needed something new to wear, Mom had to make it for us. She was so talented and smart about everything and we hardly ever had to go to a store like people do today.

Mom had me lay on the floor on top of one of grammies old coats. I would lay down with my arms straight out from my shoulders and my legs out on an angle. I could hear Mom's scissors as she cut around me. It was like I was a paper doll. When I stood up the outline of my new coat was on the floor, and it looked like me! I was so excited. Mom took the coat to the sewing machine and sewed up the seams. The sewing machine was so loud. Mom would put her feet on the large black iron peddle near the floor, which she would pump up and down. It made the needle and thread go up and down and Mom was moving the coat pieces all over the place. My coat was done in no time.

I couldn't wait to put it on. When I tried on my new coat it fit me perfectly and it was so heavy and warm with a fur collar that felt like a kitten on my face. I loved my new coat, and I didn't want to take it off.

I was the oldest, so a lot of times my clothes would be handed down to my younger sisters when I outgrew them. I always knew that they would love my special winter coat like me. I felt so lucky to have my new warm coat in those cold Maine winters.

Eight

Winters would come and we would stay warm by the wood stove. We had every blanket on our beds and it made it hard for me to move, but I loved it. Of course, Mom made them from scraps of wool.

One day while Mom was sewing, she took a scrap of material and made a doll blanket for Judy. Sharlene and I asked what can we have? Mom looked at us while thinking and went straight to her jewelry box and pulled out a necklace of large orange wooden beads and put it around Sharlene's neck! Sharlene smiled with excitement and ran off. Now, it was my turn. Yay! Mom dug deep and pulled out my grammy Alice's wedding ring. She put it on a chain and put it around my neck. I was confused. Why I was wearing it there and not on my finger? I asked Mom why and she told me how special this ring was and it will be safe on the chain.

When I went back outside to play with Judy and Sharlene, I took that necklace off and put the ring on my finger. I thought that is where rings are supposed to go, right?

I watched Judy, little Judy with her big belly and rubber pants over her diapers, walking down the dirt road. She was so cute with her little chubby legs. Then I saw a snake going down the road slowly and steadily. Its movement was so cool going back and forth and I knew I wanted to play with it so badly. I ran into the woods and found a long stick to poke at the snake to make it go faster. Oh, so fun, but then the snake went into the woods and then I noticed MY RING WAS GONE! My eyes filled up with tears while I looked up and down that dirt road and turned over every stone with my stick. I never found it! My heart was broken because I knew mom trusted me with that ring and I failed big time.

We played outside a lot in the snow. Across the road there was a hill. My teacher, Harriet Burk, was my neighbor, too, and lived on top of the hill and she would let us play there. My sisters and I would go over to the top of the hill and slide down. I found an old washing machine cover in the woods behind my house. It was round and metal. I brought it to the top of the hill and got on it and used it for a sled. It worked and it went fast, too! My sisters used cardboard boxes and we did have one actual sled. But I liked my washing machine cover. We played so much that our hands got so cold. My homemade mittens got wet, and they didn't keep my hands warm anymore, so we would go back into the house to hang out by the woodstove. Mom was mad because we came inside too soon for her liking, but we were cold. The house smelt so good from the bread that Mom was baking and the woodstove felt so good. We would dry our mittens by the stove and it would reminded me of the story that Mom would tell us about "The Three Little Kittens That Lost Their Mittens."

Our kitchen always smelt so good because every day Mom was in that kitchen cooking something for us. She knew that I loved watching her make her yeast rolls. So sometimes she would call me into the kitchen to see her do her magic and I felt so special. She would take a piece of dough from the big bowl and stick it on two of her fingers. Then she pulled it down her fingers until it was very round and smooth. She would pull it off and pinch the bottom and put them into a greased pan one by one. The pan looked like cream-colored bubbles: just so smooth and perfect. She would let them rise and boy were they delicious with a little butter on them. She was a good cook and I knew someday I would be too.

We didn't have dessert often, so Mom would give us bread with butter and sugar to eat. Yummy!! All that sugar was a little grainy in my mouth, but I loved our special treat.

When the blueberries came out, Mom would use her grandmothers recipe and make us a blueberry cake. The recipe was called "One Egg Cake." Mom just added the blueberries to it and when it came out of the oven she would put butter on the top. Because the cake was hot the butter melted and she would sprinkle the melted butter with sugar. I still make this cake today. It's so good, believe me!

My Red Sneakers

This is my Great Grammies recipe:

1 c. Sugar

3T. Crisco

1 Egg

1c. Milk

2c. Flour

Pinch of salt

1t. Vanilla

3 round t. Baking power

Bake at 350 deg. Till done

Nine

My great grandmother, Alice, loved books. She had bookcases with glass doors filled with colorful books. I didn't know how to read but, I loved to look at the pages and hunt for the pictures. I knew that my younger sister, Judy, could read and that I *should* know how to read, but the letters of the words meant nothing to me. I wondered why not? I was in school now, so why couldn't I read like my sister? Sometimes I would open the doors slowly and pull out a book. I opened it carefully and smelt the wonderful book of words as I rubbed my fingers across the pages gently. The old books were so beautiful. I loved the smell of the old books and the feel of the thin paper.

A lot of the times, in the beginning of the first chapter, the first letter of the word would be in a picture with the letter in the middle. My great grandmother would color in the pictures with colored pencils, which made it even more beautiful. I loved hunting for those letters that Grammy colored, and it always made me smile when I found one. Boy, I wish I had one of those books now! I remember one special book, a larger navy blue book with gold print on the cover. It was a book full of pictures and nursery rhymes. My mom would read from it now and then and the part that I loved the most was this one poem that read:

My Red Sneakers

"Were did I get those eyes so blue,
Out of the sky as I came through."

I knew it was about me because I had blue eyes!

Ten

I only had one pair of shoes at a time and we would have them until they wore out. I always loved red sneakers and always wanted more red sneakers. I loved how bright red was and that was all I ever wanted. RED. When I got new shoes, I wouldn't want to wear them because I wanted them to last. I loved the smell, and they were so clean and pretty. Instead, I would sleep with them on my pillow at night and when I woke up, I could see them all red and new!

In the summer, before school was starting, Dad put us in the back of the car and off to Calais we would go to get my new pair of sneakers.

My Red Sneakers

On the ride home I would be holding my new sneakers on my lap so happy and proud. Dad looked back at me and asked for my old sneakers. I took them off and gave them to him. He rolled down his window and threw them out. I was so upset to look out the back car window to see my old sneakers bouncing off the road. I started to cry and ask Dad. "Why did you do that?"

He said, "Darlene, you are lucky to have new sneakers! There might be someone poorer than us that will see those sneakers in the road and stop. They will bring them home for their little girl to wear."

This was the first time that I had heard the word POOR. What did that mean, and why are we poor when we had everything we needed.? I never forgot about that day, and I hope that if a girl did find them, that she loved those red shoes as much as I had.

Eleven

It was 1959, and I was going to first grade. I was so excited to learn new things and to be smart like the older kids were. I went to school in a two-room schoolhouse. It was heated by a woodstove. The woodstove was up front by the teacher, and it was a lot bigger than the one we had at home. I thought it was a very modern school, because the outhouse was hooked on to the building! We didn't even have to go outside to use it. This was great for when it was cold outside. I just went up front of the classroom and opened a door on the side of the room. It was so dark in there, but it didn't smell too bad. Wow, how nice!

The school desk and chairs were made out of wood and metal and all hooked to each other in a row. The smaller desks were in the front and they got bigger as they went to the back. The first grade was in the front of the class and as the kids got older, each grade was behind each other. The big kids were in the other room. I could hear the laughing and talking. My classroom was very quiet while my teacher, Mrs. Burk, was talking. She was my neighbor and I really liked her and I really like going to school.

We would play outside in the grass. I loved getting in a circle with all the big kids and playing. They seemed so smart and they had great ideas There was a wooden fence with a lot of cows on the other side of the fence. I had never seen cows so close up before, and I thought they were so big and had beautiful eyes.

One day, the fence broke, and all the cows came

into the playground!!! All the kids were screaming and running away from the cows and into
the school. It was so funny to see all the commotion. One cow tried to go into the school! It
was going up the steps and the teacher was trying to get the cows to go down the steps. I
thought it was so funny to watch. We all stayed
off to the side so the cows wouldn't run us over.
They were going very fast and the kids were
scattered and screaming and some were laughing
to see such a sight.

We had a big brass bell with a long wooden
handle. Everyone had a chance to ring it to let
the kids know that school was about to start. I
only remember ringing it once. It was very
heavy but the sound was so pretty. I was so proud
to have my chance to ring it. After I was done,
and all the kids were inside, I walked up to the
front of the school and put that bell on the
teacher's desk. She gave me a smile to let me
know that I did a good job. I was proud.

My Red Sneakers

The school was a simple white wooden building with one door and two stairways to get up to it. When we walked in the door there was an entryway with a table on the left with a big pail of spring water. There were paper cups for us to use to get a drink after recess. The cups were flat paper that we would pop open to put water in it. I thought it was nice to have my own cup. I wanted to keep it, but I didn't, because once it got wet it would get a little soggy. Oh well!

On the first day of school, I had a pencil and I always had a coloring book with a new box of crayons. When I got my schoolwork done and the teacher was teaching the older kids, I would color in my coloring book. You know I loved that!

I just loved school because it was so fun!!! Mrs. Burk loved me and she always was smiling and wore pretty clothes. She would give me As on my report card, which ended up being a problem when I went to Exeter Elementary School in 1962.

I was 9 years old, and they placed me in the smartest class in fourth grade but I didn't even know how to read yet! It wasn't good.

Back to Maine. After a couple of years going to that two-room schoolhouse, the school caught on fire and burnt to the ground. I remember my dad coming home to tell my mom that the school was on fire!!! Dad's eyes were so big when he was telling Mom. I knew it must be really a bad thing that was happening. I don't remember the time of year that this all happened, but I never went back to school until they built a new one. That was ok with me because I got to play outside with my sisters.

Sometimes I would play school and I would be the school teacher and my sisters were the students. I would make things for them to do like math problems and I would hand them out for them to do. And of course, we always colored. It was fun playing school!

The people in the town of Robbinston built a

new school for us. They were very proud of this new school. It was a brick building and all the classrooms were all on one level. There was one room for each grade. It also had a big playground with swings. The swings were different than the swings that Dad had made for me and my sisters. When I got on these new swings and started to pump my legs, I could really make it get really high in the air. It also made me feel a little sick.

The lights were very bright inside the classrooms. It kinda hurt my eyes. I didn't like that at all. Plus, the new school didn't have an outhouse. There was no wooden door like before. You had to go to a big room with bright lights and a lot of people went in at the same time. It was so loud with strange sounds of water and people moving around and talking to each other. The room was so full of echoes from everywhere. I didn't like this place at all, so I turned around and walked out. I never went in there again. I would wait until recess and went pee in the woods that was beside the playground. I knew I wasn't the only one doing this because I would see kids coming out from behind the trees. I missed my old school because things here were so different.

My father, Percy, was one of twelve children. They all had outhouses, and this was the norm. The first time I saw a "flush" (that is what they called it) was at an aunt's house. She had it in a room inside her house. I thought it was so crazy to go to the bathroom right inside your house and sit on this white porcelain seat. It was full of water that didn't come from a well. It had a handle that you would pull, and the water would leave the seat and new water would come back in. It felt so cool on my face when I pulled the string and the water was so clear. My aunt hollered to me and said, "Darlene are you wasting my water?" So I never did that again!!!

My Red Sneakers

I remember starting second grade and Sharlene was starting first grade. Mom bought us new dresses for the first day of school from the Sears catalog. I had a blue dress with flowers on it and a blue sweater. Also, pretty socks and new shoes. Sharlene had a yellow dress just like mine with a sweater and new socks and shoes too. We were like twins with our matching outfits and our coloring books and pencils.

Mom even took us to the city, Calais, and took us to a beauty store to cut and curl our hair for our first day of school. The smell in there was so strong with hair products! I didn't like it, but I was so excited to see what the hairdresser was going to do to me and Sharlene. While she was cutting my hair, I could see Mom across the room and she was smiling at me. No one had ever cut my hair but Mom. I knew this was so special. I could see Sharlene getting her hair washed in this really nice sink then she was waiting to get her hair cut after me. The lady cut our hair way too short and then decided to give us a perm. Oh no, big mistake! The perm hurt my skin around my face, and it smelt so bad it stung my eyes. My hair was full of curlers, and they put me under this helmet like thing that blew warm air on my head. I couldn't hear anything, but it was so fun to read people's lips. It was nice and warm, and I liked it and my hair dried faster! The nice lady would come and check on me often to make sure it wasn't too hot for me. I looked at Sharlene and we looked exactly alike. We both had short hair with tight curls. We looked just like twins. We had a lot of fun for sure getting ready for the first day of school. I was thinking how fun it will be to have Sharlene with me at school and we can play together.

When Sharlene and I got home boy, was Dad mad at Mom! Poor mom! He was so loud in the kitchen that I ran upstairs to get away. She didn't know that the lady was going to mess up our hair like that. She was just trying to get us ready for the beginning of school.

When I was in first grade, we had our school pictures taken. Mom curled my hair pretty that day and I wore my best clothes. I had on a little gold, heart-shaped locket that Grammy had given to me for my birthday. I was so excited about getting my picture taken!

So, I went to school in my best stuff, but they never called me to get my picture taken until after recess. You know how much I loved going outside, right? Well, being outside, it was time for me to play, and I never thought about anything but that. I went on the swings and the carousel, and you know I went as fast as I could. They rang the bell and I went inside to get my picture taken with my hair all a mess and my clothes all disheveled. I just smiled at the camera and they snapped the picture.

When they came in, Mom was very happy with

them even though I was a little messed up. Everyone in my class had a little picture of themselves to give away. So, Mom made me a little photograph book. Mom put all my classmates' pictures in this book to keep them all together. It was made of heavy construction paper held together with ribbon. I loved my photo book and I looked at it often.

Twelve

I played a game with my sisters and mom called, "Button, Button, who's got the Button?"

Mom had a button can. It was full of beautiful buttons that were all colors and all sizes. I picked out just one button that was a good size that could hide in my folding hands.

We would have one button and we would hold it between one person's hands and hold out our hands like we were praying. We stood in a circle and would slide our hands between each person's praying hands. Somewhere along the circle of sisters you would drop the button out of your hands into someone else's hands without stopping and without letting anyone know when you did it. There would be someone in the middle of the circle that had to guess who had the button and that person would be the next sister that had the button to secretly hide in someone's hands. It was so simple but so much fun. You had to be clever and have a straight face so no one could tell who had the button. I loved having Mom play with us and seeing her having fun. Mom was always working so hard taking care of everything that it was extra special having her play games with us. She had big hands and always had a hard time dropping the button without us seeing her move her hands. She always made it fun, and she would laugh a lot.

One day, in early spring, Mom had some pussy willows. She decided to do a project with us. I loved it when Mom stopped doing chores and played with us. She sat down in a chair, and we all sat around her on the floor as we watched her with wonder. She had this blue-gray heavy construction paper in one hand and a black crayon in the other. With the black crayon she drew a wooden fence with a fence post. Then she pulled off a few of the pussy willows and she glued them onto the fence. She said that they were cats setting on the fence. She then took the crayon and made a long tail, ears, and whiskers on each cat. I could see those cats come alive with every stroke of the crayon! They looked just like cats, so gray and soft and perfectly wonderful.

I loved what Mom had made them for us, and every spring we would ask her to make those pussy willow cats for us again. She always smiled and said, "Really?" and she would make them again. Each time was like the first time, and I loved seeing those little gray cats on the fence. I think Mom had an imagination like me too. We were just alike!

I also loved to play with my dolls. They were like real people to me. One day, two very nice ladies came to visit Mom. No one ever came to our home for a visit, not even my grandparents. No one. Mom was so excited to see them, and she told me they were people that she knew from long ago.

They had presents for me and my sisters. They gave me a beautiful doll! Her hair was blond and very curly. She was wearing a beautiful light-blue dress, which was my favorite color as a little girl. Her lips were red and sweet, and she had blue glass eyes with long eyelashes. So was so special to me. I never named my dolls because I couldn't remember what I named them. They were just my Dollies. I loved her and I took her with me everywhere. She wasn't a very big doll, but she had a lot of style. If I went outside, she went outside.

Well, one day I was playing outside and when it was time to go back inside for supper, I forgot to bring her in with me. The next day when I went outside I couldn't find her! She was lost and I was so sad. Where was she? I looked and looked but I couldn't find her. Overnight I would look out the window and think about her lying outside all alone. When winter came and the snow covered the ground, I would think about how cold she must be. I was so sad without her, and I never forgot about her.

When I got older, probably in my forties, I went back to where my Grammy's house used to stand. I met a man that had bought the land that the house was once on. We talked a lot about all my family that had lived there long ago. I told him stories about my family with all the little girls that lived there. I asked him if he had ever found a little doll. His eyes got big and he said, "Yes." I was so happy and very surprised. He said that his wife loves the doll and had her on their mantle. I asked if I could see her again. It had been about forty years. He said, "NO!" I told him that I won't take her but I just wanted to see her one more time, but he just wouldn't take me to his house. I couldn't believe him, and

I was shocked by his reaction and so very sad but I knew that was such a Maine thing. They are so protective, and I was now an outsider. But, I was happy to know my beloved doll was inside, safe and very loved. That made me so happy for her.

Thirteen

L iving in the deep woods of Maine, there was this library van that would come to my house. Our town didn't have a library, so this was very special. It was summer recess between second and third grade and Sharlene and I could get a book to look at for the summertime while school was out. The van was very big and white and very long. I knew this was a very special day!

It had metal steps that pulled down with handles to get inside. When I got in the van the floor was very shaky and it was so full of books! It was like nothing I had ever seen. I didn't know how to read, but I found a big book that had beautiful colored pictures of birds and flowers. It was so pretty. All summer I would sit outside with this book and look at the large pictures under a cool tree. I had never seen birds and flowers like them before and now I knew they existed, and I wanted to find them. It made me so happy to have my own book even if it was for a short time. Someday, when I was all grown up, I would have a bookcase full of books; I just knew it. At the end of the summer, the van came back and I had to give them my book back. I never saw that van again but that one time. I was thankful for that van and that book.

Fourteen

It was September of 1959, and we all were so happy because Mom was going to the hospital in Calais to have another baby!! We didn't know if we were going to have another sister or a brother. I was so excited to see the baby. Dad came home and told us that we had another sister, and her name was Debbie Kay.

Mom and Dad chose each of my sisters' names to rhyme. They thought it was cute. It went by our ages. Darlene, Sharlene, Judy Mae and Debbie Kay. My middle name is Shirley. I was named after my grandmother, my mom's mother. I always loved my name and I rhyme with Sharlene. Sharlene's middle name is Ray, but we never used it in the rhyme because we didn't need to. Mom had another baby when I was around thirteen years old. They named her Terry Faye to continue the rhyme.

Dad took us to the hospital, and we all stood in the parking lot of the hospital. Mom came to a window high up in the hospital and held Debbie so we could see her. She was so beautiful, and Mom looked so happy. We all waved to her, and Mom waved back to us. I missed her and I wanted her to come back home with us, but she had to stay at the hospital for a little longer.

When Dad came back to the car after visiting Mom, he gave me a present. It was the Bible. It was white leather with a gold zipper and a gold cross that dangled off the zipper to help open and close it. It was like nothing I had ever seen. It was so beautiful, and I felt so lucky to have it. I didn't know why he gave it to me, but he did and I loved it. When I unzipped the Bible, the pages were so thin and I would hunt for the beautiful colored pictures. There were only a few pictures here and there. One was of Moses, and one was of Noah's ark with a flying dove. They were beautiful and they were mine to look at any time. I loved my book and I always wished I could read it but I knew one day I would be able to. I had my own book, my very own for ever and ever!

When dad brought mom and Debbie home from the hospital, they had a bassinet set up in the living room. Mom put Debbie carefully in her new bed while we all looked at her. She was so beautiful with her dark hair, and she looked just like a little doll laying there so cute and quiet. She stayed inside while the rest of us went back outside to play. Dad was so very proud, and he would say, "I finally have a baby that looks just like me with those big brown eyes, dark hair and olive skin." He loved her so much through and through. When Debbie grew up it never changed and we always knew if we wanted anything we had Debbie ask Dad and he never said NO to her. We all just hung back and smiled. It worked like magic.

Fifteen

One of my problems was I talked too fast. I remember my dad looking at me and telling me to slow down. I just couldn't!! Really, Dad didn't talk to me much and he made me nervous when he did. Let's just say that Dad scared me because he had a bad temper. I wanted him to love me, and I tried to be a good girl, but I really didn't want to be that close to him. When his eyes locked onto mine it was too much, and I just wanted to run away. So, I would talk fast to be done faster and get back to playing. It worked I think but I never could change the way I talked unless I said to myself, "Take a breath and slow down."

My Red Sneakers

As a family, we didn't talk to each other about our day or really anything. We were to be seen and not heard. I only talked to my sisters and not to anyone else. Mostly, I played by myself, and my world was just perfect like that.

I know that when I moved to Exeter at nine years old everyone laughed at my Maine accent and the way I pronounced my words. So, yes, I didn't talk to them either. No way, Jose. I took a lot of special reading classes, and I always knew that the way I talked had a lot to do with my reading and spelling too.

Right up till now, I still watch people having a conversation with each other and how easy it is for them. When one person stops, the other continues. It's like a rhythm of people's words. Beautiful.

Sixteen

One time, all my sisters and I had chicken pox. Dad put black tar paper on our bedroom window so our bedroom would be dark like nighttime. We would sleep all day in our little beds and in a row. Mom told us not to scratch our bumps no matter what!! I tried so hard to do what Mom said, but I was so itchy. Me and my sisters were trying to figure out how to relieve the itchy feeling without touching and we would just laugh at ourselves. I loved Sharlene and Judy so much. We looked so funny with all those red spots. But, I did scratch one spot on my forehead and I have a divet there now. I should have done what Mom said, but I just couldn't.

It was so fun being sick all together. Our beds were so close together and in a row, so we could talk in a whisper with each other and Mom and Dad wouldn't know that we were still awake. We would talk for hours and sleep a lot in that dark room.

Dad never took the tarpaper off our windows, even when we all got better. They liked it that way because they would send us off to bed early in the summertime and we would go right to sleep. I've never outgrown the love of going to bed early and sleeping.

One night, after we were over the chicken pox, we were sent to bed but it was still light outside and I wasn't tired. I could hear Dad outside, so I tried to find a spot in the tar paper that I could peak out and see what he was doing. I found a small pin hole in it and the light was shining through. He was outside and there was this big black bear by the well!! He was making a big commotion and the bear turned around slowly and went back into the woods. After that, I was never again asked to help get pails of water from the well.

Seventeen

Dad was a hunter. If it didn't run in the woods, we didn't eat meat. We always had guns around the house, and there wasn't anything wrong with that to me. It was the norm. Dad was a great hunter but didn't do things by the book. People would come to Maine from Massachusetts and New Hampshire and look for a tour guide to take them hunting for deer and bear. Dad was their man for the job. He always got one or more for them to take home and they would get the credit with their family and friends for killing it.

I remember this one time, Dad planted this big

field full of raspberry bushes. Then, after they matured, he brought over and old outhouse building and laid it down on its side on the side of the field by the wood line. The door had a moon cutout in it so he could lay down inside and poke out the barrel of the gun. He would lay there and waited for the deer to come and eat the berries. He always got his deer, they never saw him or smelt him, and he always caught them by surprise while they were eating. It worked like a charm.

He took me there one time, and I got inside with him. It was really tight for both of us and his gun too, but it was so much fun. But nothing showed up in the field. No deer and no bear and not even a rabbit. It was ok with me because I loved animals, but I also sure loved the way they tasted!!

We also ate rabbit meat. It wasn't my favorite, but Mom would make it with a gravy, and I loved gravy. It wasn't unusual to see a deer or bear hanging upside down from a tree, waiting to be cut up. One time I helped Dad skin a big rabbit. He was kind of surprised that I wanted to help him, but I thought the inside of animals was so interesting. How everything fit so close together and perfect in every way. I held the back legs and Dad held the front of the rabbit and it took no time for the job to get done. Then we gave it to Mom to cook for supper. I asked him if I could have a back leg for a good luck charm. So he cut it off and gave it to me as a keepsake. I loved it because it was very soft.

One time, there was this old house down the hill from us and no one lived there. People in Maine didn't lock their houses up. Really, there wasn't any reason to, and no one ever carried keys with them. This house was empty, so Dad had this idea to fill this house with loose hay and rabbits. Dad would bring us down with him now and then to help him feed all the rabbits. I loved this one bunny that was so white and had big pink eyes. I always hunted for her every time when I went there with Dad. I loved it when Dad was happy, but he was so unpredictable. I wished he would always be like this, and he would let me go with him and we could have fun together. There were a lot of rabbits, but only this one white bunny and she was mine. I loved trying to catch her so I could hold her and pat her, but she was so fast!!

Well, with time the rabbits multiplied, and the house was full of rabbits of all sizes. I loved going down to that house with Dad to see the rabbits. They would be sleeping and hiding in the hay, so I had to walk carefully not to step on any baby bunnies.

Then one day Dad opened the door to let all the rabbits out!!! It took a while for them to understand that the door was opened. We sat up on the hill and watched the field beside the house fill up with hopping rabbits. They must have been so happy to be outside in the sun. It was such a beautiful sight. I was so happy to be a part of such joy and excitement.

One day when I was in my forties, Sharlene told me that the rabbit that I had happily helped Dad cut up for supper had been my pet bunny. I was shocked and I had no idea. Nonelll So all those rabbits in that old abandoned house were for us to eat? Really? Oh no, that was awful, but kinda brilliant at the same time too.

We also had a lot of chickens running around the yard. Dad now and then would kill one so we could have chicken to eat for supper. He would cut off their heads and hang them by their feet on the clothesline. I was watching when one chicken fell off and started to run around with no head. I started to laugh so hard because the chicken was running in circles and kept falling over. It was so funny, and I couldn't stop laughing at the sight of all those poor chickens. Dad was so mad at me laughing and he told me to stop but I just couldn't. So he told me to go into the house and I went but I still thought it was funny.

Another time, Dad went fishing but not the usual way with a fishing pole. He brought dynamite to the river and threw it in. It killed all the fish and they all floated to the top and he scooped them up and filled two pails to the top with fresh fish!!! He went to his brothers' and sisters' houses and gave them some fish and we had fish for supper that night. He was laughing so hard about his catch, but he thought he wouldn't do that again.

Eighteen

I was very sick with measles, and I was laying on the couch in the living room. Mom and Dad were very scared for me because I had a high fever and was hallucinating that there were bugs climbing up the wall. I don't remember much after that, but Mom and Dad took me to the hospital. I do remember waking up in this bright room with beautiful women wearing white, looking down at me and smiling. I thought I was in heaven!!! It was so bright and white, and my bed had white sheets and I was so comfortable. I had this rubber doll beside me. She had the sweetest face, and her clothes were a part of her body.

I looked around and I realized that I was in a hospital and those beautiful women were nurses. I didn't want to go home but Mom and Dad came to get me and take me home. The nurses let me keep the rubber doll because they knew how much I loved her. They told Dad that it was a good thing that they had brought me to the hospital when they did, because I could of died. When I heard that I thought I must have been very sick but I felt great now.

My grandmother, Alice, died and Mom was very sad. She loved her so much. Dad took us to see her for the last time in this big building in the city. We all walked in and Grammy was laying there and it looked like she was sleeping. I never saw her all dressed up before because she was always in her cotton nightgowns and robes. Boy, she looked so beautiful in her bed, which was mauve pink velvet and her dress matched.

My Red Sneakers

When I looked around, the chairs had satin material and the curtains had tassels. Grammy had to be in heaven because it all was so beautiful. I really loved my grammy and I knew I was going to miss her very much.

Her favorite flowers were lilacs, so every Memorial Day we would pick her a bouquet and put them in a vase and bring them over to her grave. We placed them by her big beautiful tall headstone. It was so big, with her name written in fancy lettering. Grammy would have loved that we did that for her, I thought.

I always said my prayers before I went to bed. I got on my knees and put my praying hands on the bed. I said the prayer that Mom taught me:

Now I lay me down to sleep

I pray the Lord my soul to keep

If I die before I wake

I pray the Lord my soul to take

God Bless.......

My Red Sneakers

I blessed my mom and dad, my sisters and then always said; "Amen!"

I used to wonder, why did it say "If I die before I wake"? I'm not going to die in bed! That's just crazy.

Nineteen

I loved Christmas at my house with my sisters. We were so excited that Santa was coming and we would get presents. All I wanted was a baby doll. Dad would get a Christmas tree from outside in the woods and bring it home so we could put it in the living room. It would make the house smell so good.

Dad would put the Christmas lights on the tree and it looked so colorful with all those colored bulbs. I would put on the silver tinsel only two to three pieces at a time. It took forever but that is the way Mom wanted it done. When the mail came, and we got Christmas cards, we would put them on the tree for decorations.

At nighttime, when it was dark outside, I would lay under the Christmas tree with all the lights on. I lay with my head looking up through the tree, looking at all the colors. Mom and Dad had some lights that even had this liquid in it that made these little bubbles that moved up and down this tube-shaped part of the light. The heat of the lights made the tree smell so good. I loved laying there along with Sharlene and Judy. We sang Christmas songs from the ones we learned at Church. It was such a wonderful time.

On Christmas morning, Santa would put each of our Christmas stockings by the foot of our beds. We all were so excited to open them. I loved my Christmas stocking because it used to be Mom's when she was a little girl. We couldn't go downstairs until Mom and Dad said we could. Then, we would all run down the stairs and see all the presents. I got new slippers with a dog head on the toe of each slipper. They were so soft and cozy, and the dog's head moved with each step. I loved my new slippers and yes, I got a new baby doll and even a tea set. Mom would cook us a big dinner of chicken because Dad hated turkey. The house smelt so good, and everyone was so happy, playing and eating together. I loved Christmas time!!!!

Twenty

O n Sundays, my sisters and I would go to church. I loved walking up the road to-gether, holding hands and talking and even sometimes singing church songs. There was a small white church on top of the hill with this big steeple and large wooden doors. Inside would be the sounds of beautiful music and talking people so happy to see us coming inside. I loved it there because I always felt loved. We would talk about all the Bible stories and color pictures. Before it was time to go back home, they would give me a card with a beautiful Bible verse on one side with a picture on the other. When I got home, I would put my card in my bureau drawer with all the others that I had saved. I often pulled them out and looked at all the pretty pictures and thought how lucky I was.

I went to church one day before Christmas and it was so pretty and it smelt so good inside. People sang Christmas songs, and everyone sang along with them. I had so much fun that day. The minister asked us if we had anything that we wanted to say. I raised my hand up and he looked at me and smiled and asked if I wanted to say something. I told him that I wanted to sing. So I got up front and stood beside him and looked at all the smiling faces looking at me. I was so happy and started singing a song to everyone. It was called, "I'm Dreaming of a White Christmas." People said that they liked my song and I felt so proud. When I sang at my church at that moment, I had no fear. I just was so happy and excited. I loved all the people's smiles looking at me. My mom and dad never went to church with us, and no one made me feel bad and told me to shut up and be silent. My church wanted to hear me and love me.

I have always felt very close to God and I knew that Jesus loved me very much. I wasn't just a person in a crowd, but I was known as Darlene and that I was a special little girl that was loved very much. He knew me by name, and he cared about me very much. I always knew that I was never alone and not to worry about anything because he was there.

When I was little, one of my first memories was of me looking down the narrow and very steep staircase. I would stand on the top and wonder why I couldn't go down without walking down. I don't mean sliding down on my bum. I mean just willing my way down to the bottom of the stairs. I knew that I used to be able to do this and why not now? I knew if I jumped, I would fall and hurt myself. I remembered there was a time, a place that I was at, that I could do just that without effort. I thought that I hated feeling so heavy! I didn't know why things had to be like this. It really troubled me, and I thought about it a lot. Why was everything just so different now? It never used to be this way. I went outside and got on top of the doghouse and stood there for a while; wishing I could get off the roof without jumping. But, I couldn't!!! Nothing worked, so I got on my hands and knees and sadly climbed down. After a while I really never thought about it again. Those times were gone. But, I never stopped believing in the love that surrounded me.

I've always known that I'm a spiritual being having a human experience.

I have always wondered, "Why don't people around me believe in that power and love of God?"

I brought that love with me throughout my life. I realized early in life that it was never money and things that made me happy but it has always been the feeling of that love in my heart. I have grown to understand that I can't make people see the world like me, so I just give them unconditional love and kindness and I try to let them know they aren't alone in this world.

Darlene

Dad with Darlene and pet crow

Darlene in first grade

Mom with Sharlene, Judy, and Darlene

Dad with Darlene and Sharlene

Mom pregnant with Debbie.
Darlene, Judy, and Sharlene

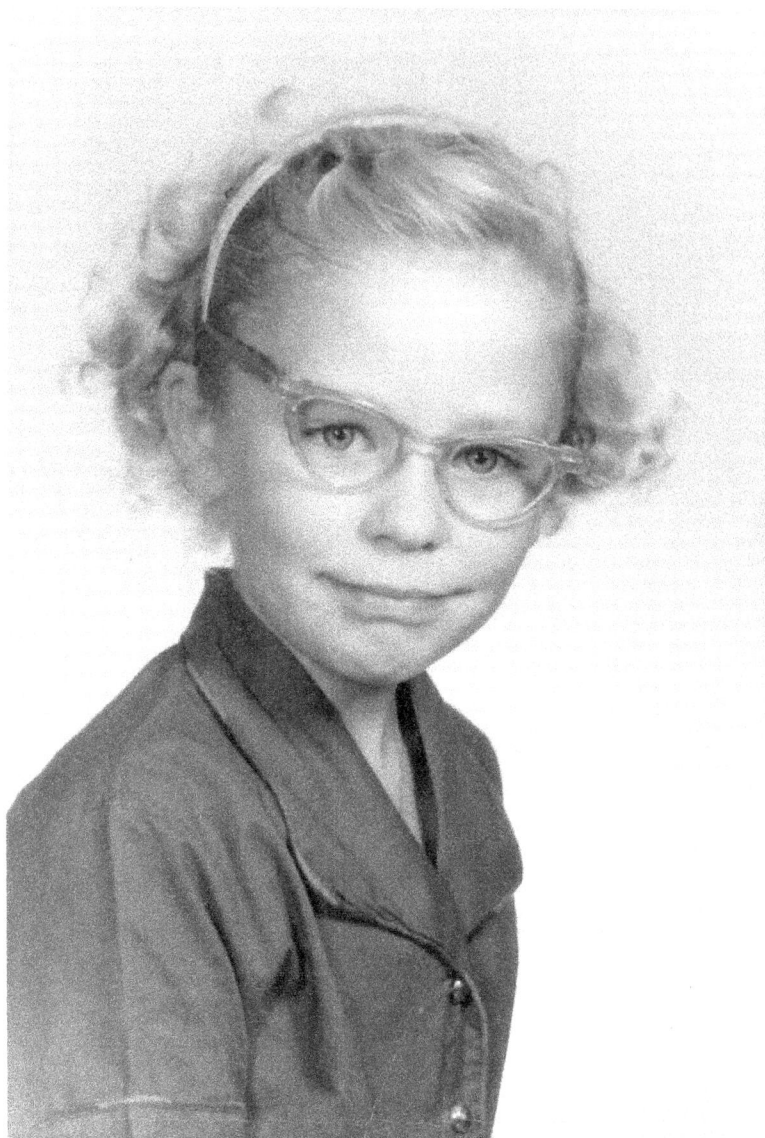

Darlene in third grade

www.ingramcontent.com/pod-product-compliance
Lightning Source LLC
Chambersburg PA
CBHW041012140426

R18136500001B/R181365PG42813CBX00013B/3/J

9781958669198